Between Self and Parts:
A 30-Day Journey of Self-Discovery with
The U Model™:
ACT & IFS
Who's truly in charge?
Find the hidden hand
and
The *Self*.

Dr. Rivka Edery, Psy.D, LCSW

Praise for Between Self and Parts:
A 30-Day Journey of Self-Discovery with ACT & IFS

'*Dr. Rivka Edery's Between Self and Parts: A 30-Day Journey of Self-Discovery with ACT & IFS is a masterful blend of Internal Family Systems and Acceptance and Commitment Therapy, offering a clear, compassionate path to self-discovery. Her internal family system metaphor invites readers of all backgrounds to explore their inner world with kindness. This journal is a gift for anyone seeking purpose and peace.*' -Alice Rizzi, PsyD

'*Between Self and Parts is a thoughtful and affirming guide for navigating complexity with curiosity, compassion, and clarity. A much-needed bridge between parts work and values-based living.*'

- Helen Dempsey-Henofer, LCSW

'*As a practitioner, I deeply appreciate the elegant clarity Dr. Edery brings to the complex landscape of the mind. Between Self and Parts is a remarkable internal family system, crafted within these pages, that beautifully demystifies the inner workings of our inner world. This brilliant, hands-on journal weaves together ACT and IFS with compassionate prose and actionable exercises, actively guiding you to reshape your inner world and step into your true Self. It's an empowering and transformative journey, offering accessible tools for profound self-discovery and leading a life aligned with purpose.*' - Josh Spell, MSW, LICSW

'Dr. Rivka Edery created this inspiring journal inclusive of self-discovery, self-acceptance, and self-love. Couched in the principles of Acceptance and Commitment Therapy (ACT) and Internal Family Systems (IFS), it offers a portal to seeking inner peace and living a more fulfilling life. Integrating inventories and worksheets and learning tools and skills to befriend your inner critic, embracing your vulnerabilities, and aligning your actions with your values will transform your relationship with yourself and others. Your 30 days of effort will undoubtedly create the results you're looking for!' -Michelle P. Maidenberg, Ph.D., MPH, LCSW-R, CGP

'*This book is more of a transformative experience than it is a book. I never expected to call my inner critic a good friend, yet I now can.*' -Christine W. Skow, MA, LMHC

'*Dr. Edery's Between Self and Parts provides thought provoking questions and assessments that are beneficial in guiding self-exploration.*' -Carrie L. E. Wendt

'*Dr. Rivka Edery's unique publication, blending ACT and IFS, offers a compassionate guide for self-discovery and gentle healing through journaling and support. Heartfelt congratulations on this labour of love destined to empower countless individuals to unburden their minds and foster lasting transformation. Well done!*' -Loretta Crawford, R.S.W., ECDCS CGP CCTP II

Between Self

and Parts:

A 30-Day Journey of Self-Discovery

with

The U Model™:

ACT & IFS

Who's truly in charge?
Find the hidden hand
and
The Self

©Dr. Rivka Edery, Psy.D, LCSW

Between Self and Parts: A 30-Day Journey of Self-Discovery with ACT & IFS
Published by *Edery House Press*
Copyright © Rivka Edery 2025
All rights reserved.
The moral rights of the author have been asserted.

E-book ISBN: 979-8-9995774-0-5
Paperback ISBN: 979-8-9995774-1-2

Printed and bound in the United States
Interior design: Edery House Press
U-Model™ diagram and design © Rivka Edery 2025, *Edery House Press*.

Dedication

For my beloved sister, Malka M. Edery:

This book is yours - a tender, creative map of the mind's inner family, guiding us through Self-Energy to the gentle release of unburdening.

Your radiant spirit, eternally dancing within these pages, has shaped my path with love and playful curiosity.

Yet my heart carries an endless grief

a quiet ache for the space where you once stood.

May this work cradle your beautiful Soul, whether you rest in *The Lavender's* tender embrace or walk unseen among us still.

אני אוהבת אותך לעד -I love you always.

You are woven into the fabric of my heart,

forever entwined in our shared soul-story.

I hold fast to the promise that we will meet again,

laughing and talking for hours, as only we could.

My Baby Sister Malky:

Seeing you in my memories heals me and tears me apart.

You are the love you see in my eyes.

Your big sister,

Rivka

Table of Contents

INTRODUCTION

Welcome to Your 30-Day Journey!

Have you ever experienced this sense of internal contradiction, as if one part of you is moving forward and another is pulling you back, caught in self-doubt, worry, or impulsive reactivity? This internal tug-of-war is profoundly human, and this journal will serve as your guide to inner peace. Imagine your mind as a busy internal family, with different members playing different roles and having distinctly different feelings, goals, and roles. Internal Family Systems (IFS) is a gentle approach to understanding this inner world, founded by Dr. Richard Schwartz. It introduces what I call *Niggle Parts* (managers who plan and organize to keep you safe, like cautious architects) and *Skitch Parts* (firefighters who move quickly to try to dampen emotional suffering, like earnest defenders). Some of them are tender, and I call them *VelFire* (Exiles, bearing old wounds of shame or fear, but glowing with healing potential). At the center of this family is your Self, a peaceful, loving, wise core that leads with calm, curiosity, clarity, compassion, confidence, courage, creativity, and connection (the 8 C's of Self).

To aid your Self in helping the various parts in this, Acceptance and Commitment Therapy, or ACT (pronounced like "act"), offers robust, evidence-based tools. ACT views thoughts as fleeting clouds and emotions as changing weather, anchoring you in the present. ACT guides you in developing psychological flexibility, leading to your deepest values - whether connection, courage, kindness, family, or something else - and to act in accordance with them.

The U-Model™: The U-Model™ integrates Internal Family Systems (IFS) and Acceptance and Commitment Therapy (ACT) into a clear, three-phase journey of self-discovery and healing. Picture a U-shaped path: you descend to meet your inner parts, connect with empathy at the base, and ascend to lead a values-driven life with your compassionate Self.

- Descent (Days 1–10): Explore and understand your protector parts (Managers and Firefighters) and their roles using IFS awareness and ACT presence.

- Empathy (Days 11–20): Offer compassionate healing to your wounded parts (Exiles) with IFS empathy and ACT acceptance, fostering connection.

- Ascent (Days 21–30): Lead your inner system with Self, aligning actions with your core values through IFS integration and ACT committed action.

Visual Note: Imagine a U-shaped path. The left side descends as you meet your parts, the base rests in empathy, and the right side ascends as you live your values with Self-leadership.

This journal invites you to make your own U-turns, transforming an internal conflict into a flexible perspective.

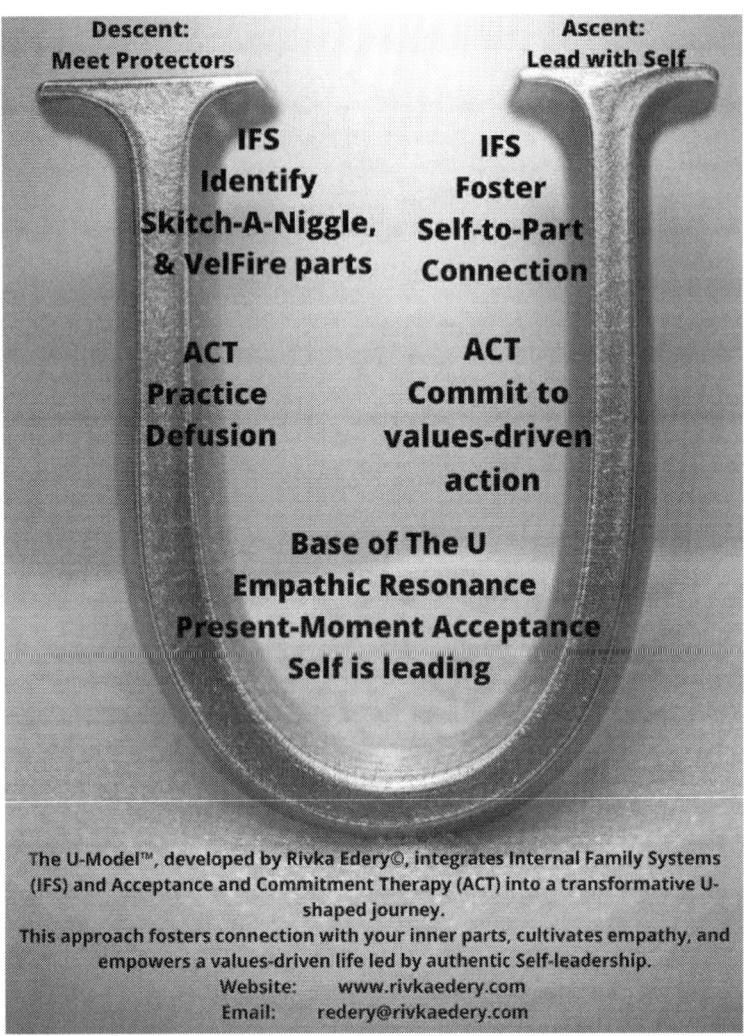

Why This Journal?

This book is born of a desire to share the tools that reshaped my life and my work as a therapist. Whether you're new to self-exploration, in therapy, or a seasoned practitioner, this journal offers accessible tools for all. Exploring these 30 days of simple, creative, 10-15-minute-a-day exercises creates a connection with your *Niggle, Skitch,* and *VelFire* parts. Intentionally secular and neurodivergent-friendly, it includes optional spiritual reflections and invites you to proceed at your own pace. All you need is a pen, a quiet moment, and an open heart. Get a warm drink, get comfortable, and let's get started.

Your inner family is waiting, and your Self is poised to be the loving leader your parts have been waiting for!

-Rivka Edery

June 2025

Part I: Approaching Your Internal Family System

Welcome to Your Inner Family

Welcome to Your Inner Family

Imagine your mind as a haven nestled on a windswept hill. Within its walls, a radiant child, your most authentic Self, thrives. Managers (whom I call 'Niggle Parts') patrol the edges, planning to keep threats at bay. Firefighters (whom I call 'Skitch Parts') stand ready at the gates, rushing to quell emotional sparks, while exiled parts, tucked in quiet corners, carry old sorrows (whom I call 'VelFire').

I coined '*Skitch-A-Niggle*' to capture the playful, persistent nature of our inner manager and firefighter parts, drawing from 'skitch' (to hitch or tug) and 'niggle' (a slight, nagging feeling). The term '*Skitch-A-Niggle*' is designed to be a playful, therapeutic tool.

Above it all stands your Self, a calm, kind guide who sees each protector's burden and the inner child's innate strength. This 30-day journey, blending *Internal Family Systems* (IFS) and *Acceptance and Commitment Therapy* (ACT), invites you to explore your inner family, meet your parts, and lead with openness to create a life of purpose and meaning. I termed it: *The U Model™*. The power of the U Model lies in its robust framework for acknowledging exile pain, connecting with protective parts that maintain the holding pattern of thoughts and behaviors, and allowing the Self to be the key for the entire inner family.

This journal is for anyone curious about themselves—whether you're new to self-help, currently in therapy, or simply seeking deeper personal growth. Prior knowledge of these two modalities is preferable. A bibliography and resource list are provided at the end of this book, listing books and resources on both modalities. Feel free to check these out now if you are unfamiliar with IFS or ACT. However, I'll guide you with simple, accessible tools as we journey through the next 30 days.

One of the 'big sells' about IFS and ACT is teaching you to listen to your parts with kind, non-judgmental presence. Through ongoing practice, you recognize and accept that ALL your parts are here to stay, for as long as you live. None is going anywhere. So is your Self-Energy. Psychological flexibility skills development helps protector parts step back, nurturing trust in the Self. Flexibility includes present-moment awareness and values-based, committed action. The pathway towards less polarization (extreme of each other, not 'getting along', disagreeing, like a family in conflict) is through inner sensing presence. Your self-energy is the healing elixir.

Inner Presence, Self-Leadership, and Self-Energy provide a unique sense of peace and stability. Using focusing, felt sensing, and genuine curiosity helps you connect with your parts. Some parts are pre-verbal and express themselves through the felt sense and somatic experiencing. With time and patience - not force - your calm curiosity leads to a pivot in self-to-part connection.

I found inner peace through this method. Despite everything that has happened in my life, and during this workbook writing, this process increased my confidence. I am confident this journey will guide, teach, and inspire you, too.

What You'll Find Here

Part I: You'll learn the basics of IFS and ACT, begin to meet your inner parts, and prepare with tools like the **Parts Flexibility Inventory (PFI)** and **Self-Connection Inventory (SCI)**. You will find the complete **Parts Flexibility Inventory** and **Self-Connection Inventory (SCI)** twice. The first is before Day One, and then again in Part III, at the end of this 30-day journey.

Part II: This is the core of your journey - 30 daily prompts designed to help you connect with your hard-working protectors and their radiant inner child.

Descent: Meeting Your Protectors (Days 1–10)

This section, Descent, is dedicated to meeting Managers and Firefighters. On Manager-focused days (like Day 3, 4, & 5): When the prompt asks you to explore a Manager (e.g., a Worrier, Planner, or Critic), you will focus on one of your Niggle Parts. Sample dialogue questions might be: *"What are you worried about? What do you want me to know?"*

On Firefighter-focused days (like Day 6, 7, 8, & 9): When the prompt refers to a Firefighter (e.g., an impulsive, distracting, or reactive part), you will focus on one of your Skitch Parts. Sample dialogue questions for them might be: *"What are you trying to show me or protect me from?"*

Empathy: Healing Your Exiles (Days 11–20)

This section focuses on Exiles, the *VelFire* parts your skitches and niggles are protecting.

Sample dialogue questions for them might be: **How do my skitch parts react when this Exile's pain shows up? What about my Niggle parts?**

Ascent: Leading with Self (Days 21–30)

The focus is on harmonizing the relationship between your skitch and niggle parts, helping them work together under the leadership of your core Self.

Each day offers one to two simple exercises, typically taking 10-15 minutes. You can use a pen and paper, a digital app, or simply your imagination. Let's approach your internal system with openness and curiosity. The path begins!

Part III: Here, you'll reflect on your progress and celebrate your growth.

Understanding IFS

To navigate your inner family system, it is helpful to understand its structure. Internal Family Systems Therapy (IFS) views your mind as multi-modal (more than one part). Different "parts" play specific roles in protecting your exiled parts and keeping your functioning.

Managers (Niggle Parts: The mind's CEO and Commander-in-Chief): These parts are proactive bosses, planners, and organizers, working to keep you safe and avoid perceived dangers (e.g., controlling or critical parts to prevent rejection).

Firefighters (Skitch Parts: Distractors-in-Chief): These parts react quickly and intensely to douse emotional pain or distress (e.g., a part distracting you with endless social media scrolling to avoid feelings of inadequacy).

Exiles (VelFire: Carriers-of-Shame): These parts carry old hurts, traumas, or complex emotions such as shame or fear, often tucked away in quiet, hidden corners of your internal system (e.g., a part feeling "unworthy" due to a past, unresolved critical experience).

Self: This is your essence - a state of inherent wisdom, curiosity, and calm. *The Self is the natural, gentle guide that can lead your inner system. It is the key that unlocks healing.*

IFS helps you understand each part's positive, protective intentions. Also, it teaches you to lead your inner world from your wise and compassionate Self.

Here is one way to conceptualize the IFS approach: **Exiles hold the pain, Protectors maintain the holding pattern, and Self is the key.**

The heart of the IFS approach: Six Change-Processes

Identify Parts: Recognize the various parts of the psyche, including Exiles, Managers, and Firefighters, each with distinct functions, emotions, and beliefs.

Accessing the Self: Stepping into attributes such as calm, clarity, curiosity, compassion, confidence, courage, creativity, and choice, to promote healing.

Unburdening Exiles: A process helping hurting parts (Exiles) transform painful emotions, traumas, or limiting beliefs/perspectives, by experiencing compassionate presence.

Self-to-Part Connection: Through self-leadership, parts begin to trust you for the first time, starting to feel safe and heard.

Depolarizing Parts: Fostering agreement between parts in opposition (e.g., between a Manager and a Firefighter) to bring unity within the internal system.

Facilitating Self-Leadership: Reinforcing the Self's position as a caring leader for the parts, fostering balance and integration.

Let's look at the 'codes' that Managers, Firefighters, and Exiles live by, and suggested phrases to validate them.

Why These Validating Phrases Work with Parts

1. Heartfelt Partnership: Offer a tender invitation to connect to parts, honoring their role without judgment or dismissal.
2. Soul-Deep Resonance: Speak directly to the core of each part's struggle, mirroring their emotions with vivid, compassionate language.
3. Trust in Self: Evoke trust by weaving curiosity and care, guiding parts toward healing with Self's gentle strength.
4. Exiles hold the pain, Protectors maintain the holding pattern, and Self is the key.

For Managers (Proactive Protectors)

'A world built of order over overwhelm. A fortress against the memory of what happens when control is lost. A place we can never go back to.'

1. *I see your tireless vigil, guarding my heart from chaos. Your strength humbles me. Can I hold the reins for a moment?*
2. *Your fear whispers of disasters you've fought alone. I'm here now, fierce and steady. Will you let me stand with you?*
3. *You've woven a shield of control through endless storms. Let Love carry the weight, dear protector.*

For Firefighters (Reactive Protectors)

'Desperation is born in the chronic inferno. We will douse the flames at all costs. The escape is all that matters.'

1. *You blaze into battle to smother my pain, my selfless, fearless warrior. I'm here, unburned, ready to face the fire with you.*
2. *In your wild rush to save me, I feel your desperate heart. I'm not leaving you in this inferno. Can we pause together?*
3. *You dive into chaos to keep my wounds at bay. I see your courage. Will you trust my light to soothe the flames?*

For Exiles (Wounded Inner Children)

Exiles hold the pain, Protectors maintain the holding pattern, and Self is the key.

1. *It's not your fault.*
2. *I believe you.*

3. *You've carried this aching loneliness in the dark too long. I am beside you now, and always.*
4. *Your hidden story trembles in my heart. Speak, sweet one. I'm here listening, believing every word.*

The heart of the ACT approach: Six Change-Processes

Acceptance and Commitment Therapy (ACT), helps you live a meaningful and purposeful life by embracing your thoughts and feelings rather than fighting them. Its core processes are:

Acceptance: Openly welcoming emotions and sensations without resistance (e.g., noticing anxiety without trying to push it away).

Defusion: Seeing thoughts as just words or mental events, not absolute truths, allowing them to pass like clouds (e.g., observing the thought "I'm a failure" as simply a thought, rather than rules to obey).

Presence: Grounding yourself and staying engaged in the present moment, rather than dwelling on the past or worrying about the future.

Observing Self: Connecting to the unchanging part of you that observes your thoughts and feelings, distinct from the ever-changing roles your mind plays.

Values: Identifying what truly matters to you deep down - your core desires for how you want to live (e.g., connection, courage, kindness).

Committed Action: Taking consistent action toward your values, even when discomfort, doubt, or fear arises.

This journey integrates IFS and ACT, guiding you to explore the parts of your system (IFS) and develop psychological flexibility (ACT). We'll use *the U-Model™: An Integrated Approach to Therapeutic Transformation (IFS + ACT)*, my U-letter visual representation of this beautiful journey:

Descent (top left side of U): This initial phase involves meeting and understanding your protectors who work tirelessly for their exiles, and you ('felt sensing').

Empathy (decent to the base of U): While being in a state of Presence, you experience radical, empathic acceptance for all your parts (self-to-part connection).

Ascent (top right of the U): You lead from Self, creating a values-driven partnership. An authentic, meaningful life - not led by blended parts - by the healing, flexible Self-Energy that is innate in everyone.

Meeting Your Protectors

To introduce you to your parts, we will set the stage with the **Parts Flexibility Inventory (PFI)** and the **Self-Connection Inventory (SCI)**.

Parts Mapping Exercise - Exploring your *Skitch-a-Niggle* and VelFire

Materials: Paper and pen, or a digital app (e.g., Notes, a journaling app).

Self-Led Questions

1.   Find a quiet space where you won't be disturbed. Take three deep, settling breaths.

2.   Recall a recent emotional moment or interaction-it could be a time of stress at work, a joyful moment with friends, or a frustrating conversation.

3.   As you recall this moment, notice any thoughts, feelings, or actions that arose. Did a protector part urge you to "stay organized" or "be prepared"? (Niggle Part).

4.   Did a firefighter part push you to avoid the situation, distract yourself, or react impulsively? (Skitch Part).

5.   Did a wounded part whisper something like "I'm not enough", "I am so alone", "no one believes me", or "who will love me?" (VelFire).

6.   Write or draw these parts. Give them a name that feels right (e.g., "The Planner," "The Distractor," "The Critic").

7.   Now, from a place of curiosity, ask each identified part: "What are you protecting? What's your job?" Note the responses (e.g., Planner: 'I prevent chaos and failure'; "Distractor: 'I prevent overwhelming anxiety').

8.   Reflect: "What do I notice about how these parts interact?" Example: During a work deadline, my 'niggle' protector seemed to take over. When I asked it what it was doing, it said, "*I plan obsessively to avoid failure.*"

Accessible Option: If writing or drawing feels challenging, simply list one part and its general role, record a short voice memo describing it, or think aloud about its protective intention. For creating vision boards, consider using Canva or Pinterest.

Emotional Safety: If a part's emotions feel overwhelming, pause, take three deep breaths, and say, '*I'm here, and I'm safe.*' If needed, consult a therapist (see Resources).

Troubleshooting: If You Feel Stuck: Try a simpler exercise, like naming one feeling or part. If emotions feel intense, pause and ground yourself with the *Five Senses Check-In* (Day 4).

Quick Start Guide: IFS sees your mind as a family of parts (Managers, Firefighters, Exiles) led by your wise Self. ACT helps you accept thoughts and feelings while acting in accordance with your values. This journal combines them to guide you toward inner peace

Parts Flexibility Inventory (PFI)

The PFI is a 12-item measure of your flexibility in relation to your parts-Managers, Firefighters, and Exiles.

There are four questions for each type, and for each question, the score ranges from 1 (Strongly Disagree) to 5 (Strongly Agree), resulting in a total score of 4-20 per type and 12-60 across all three types.

The more you score, the greater your flexibility becomes in detached witnessing of your parts, rather than being dominated by them. Low scores indicate potential areas for development.

Fill in the PFI on Days 1, 16, and 30, and record your scores in the table at the bottom.

PFI Questions: Please indicate the extent to which you agree or disagree with the statements by rating them from 1 (Strongly Disagree) to 5 (Strongly Agree).

Managers (Proactive protectors focused on control and safety – the Niggle)

1. I can recognize my controlling thoughts as just thoughts, not commands

2. I can appreciate the protective intent behind my perfectionistic tendencies

3. I can act with self-compassion when I feel internal pressure

4. I feel confident in my abilities, even when a part of me fears failure

Firefighters (Reactive protectors driven by impulse to numb pain – the Skitch)

5. I can pause before acting on an impulse, like anger or craving

6. I can stay present with discomfort without needing to escape it

7. I can approach my reactive impulses with kindness and curiosity

8. I can find a sense of calm within me during an emotional storm

Exiles (Young, vulnerable parts holding pain and trauma – the VelFire)

9. I feel compassion toward the most hurt parts of myself

10. I can listen to my painful emotions without judging them

11. I am curious about my past experiences and inner world

12. I feel hopeful that my wounded parts can heal over time

Self-Connection Inventory (SCI)

The SCI is a five-item tool that assesses your connection to your Self - the calm, compassionate center that guides your internal system.

Each question can be rated from 1 (Strongly Disagree) to 5 (Strongly Agree) with a possible total score = 5-25.

Higher scores indicate stronger Self-leadership.

Fill out the SCI on Days 1, 16, and 30 and record your scores in the table.

SCI Questions: Please rate each item from 1 (Strongly Disagree) to 5 (Strongly Agree).

1. I feel calm when I observe my internal parts without judgment
2. I approach my parts with curiosity and compassion
3. I can stay present with my parts even during challenging moments
4. I trust my ability to lead my parts with confidence and clarity
5. I make conscious choices to foster connection and creativity within my inner system

Scoring and Tracking

Fill in both inventories on Day 1 (initial reflection), Day 16 (a reflection halfway through your journey), and Day 30 (your final review), with the questions above.

Keep track of your tallies in the tracking table provided. You can use a pencil or keep score in a digital app for convenience.

After every inventory, ask: "What do my scores tell me about my relationship with my parts and my Self today?" Stronger scores indicate Flexibility (PFI) & Self-connection (SCI). Every score is helpful.

Do not judge your results; instead, approach them with curiosity, as they inform you of your self-to-part connection.

Table Tracking

Parts Flexibility Inventory (PFI) and Self-Connection Inventory (SCI)

Use this table to score your PFI and SCI on Days 1, 16, and 30. These are baseline insights about your internal system. The higher the scores, the more flexibility you have with parts, and the greater Self-connection - though all scores contain information about your development. After each entry, ask yourself: *"What are my scores telling me about my relationship to my parts and my Self today?"*

DAY	MANAGERS	FIREFIGHTERS	EXILES	SELF-CONNECTION
1	4-20	4-20	4-20	5-25
16	4-20	4-20	4-20	5-25
30	4-20	4-20	4-20	5-25

Example: Day 1 Managers Score: 12 (3+3+3+3).

I noticed I struggle to see controlling thoughts as just thoughts, so I'll focus on defusion exercises.
Reflection: What's one thing I learned about my parts or Self today? Even a 1-point increase shows growth-celebrate it!

How to Use This Journal

Each day in Part II follows a similar structure to guide your journey. They will include a variation of these:

Theme: Highlights the core ACT or IFS concept and the specific type of part you'll be exploring that day.

Purpose: Clearly states the goal of the day's exercise.

Introduction: A brief narrative sets the context, often including a personal anecdote or a universal experience (e.g., workplace stress, parenting challenges, or friendship dynamics) to illustrate the day's theme in action.

Exercise: Provides step-by-step instructions, suggested materials, and options for diverse needs, to inspire your own inner conversations.

Reflection: Includes a relevant PFI or SCI question to prompt deeper introspection, a "Self-Check" question to encourage immediate self-awareness, and a "Flexibility Option" for days when a specific part might not be active.

IFS Journal Prompt: Use a separate notebook, digital app, or voice recorder to capture your responses, tailoring the experience to your needs. You have a choice, according to your preference, of writing, drawing, or simply imagining your inner family.

U-Model™ **Connection:** A brief note linking the day's practice to your overall journey through the Descent, Empathy, or Ascent phases.

Feel free to skip days, revisit exercises, or spend more time on a topic that resonates deeply with you. If you get stuck with any part, experiencing intense, uncomfortable emotions, play this mantra in your head, write it down, or use your voice to record: *"I am not my parts, and my parts aren't me."*

Make your journey a gentle, nurturing, open, and playful one.

Disclaimer: This 30-day journal is not a substitute for individual counseling. Please seek a licensed, competent, trustworthy, safe provider for personal support. You are not alone. Your healing is deepened in safe spaces and community.

Part II: The 30-Day Journey

Descent: Meeting Your Protectors (Days 1–10)

Exiles hold the pain, Protectors maintain the holding pattern, and Self is the key.

Day 1: Meet Your Manager Parts (Proactive Protectors)

Introduction: Welcome to Day 1! If you haven't already, please complete the full PFI and Self-Connection Inventory as your first task before proceeding.

Purpose: Introduction to the proactive Manager parts

Focus On: Manager Parts are hardworking, **pro**active protectors, similar to Firefighters (**re**active hardworking protectors). In their burdened state, they are stressed, hardworking, and blended. They genuinely believe that the past will repeat itself unless they prevent and control it.

The Manager's Creed

Managers act as inner bodyguards, proactively controlling your life to prevent emotional chaos. They stand guard over your Exiles - the vulnerable, childlike parts of you that hold the overwhelming pain of past wounds.

- *Never again. We must control everything to prevent that pain from surfacing.*
- *Stay vigilant, be perfect, and don't show any vulnerability.*
- *Safety comes from being prepared and staying one step ahead of any threat.*
- *A world built of order over overwhelm.*
- *A fortress against the memory of what happens when control is lost.*
- *A place we can never go back to.*

Core Beliefs:

1. Control is safety
2. Vulnerability is dangerous
3. Perfection prevents criticism, pain, abandonment
4. Logic must override emotion every time

Validation:

Take a moment to consider your hardworking managers. From a place of spacious awareness, offer heartfelt partnership to them.

Extend a tender invitation to honor their role without judgment or dismissal.

Validation speaks directly to the core of each part's struggle.

Such phrases mirror parts' emotions with vivid, compassionate language.

It evokes trust by weaving together curiosity, connection, calm, and integrity. It offers the Self's gentle strength.

When you say these statements out loud, notice and name any reactions or shifts within yourself. Feel free to write your own and use the ones that land best with your system.

I see your tireless vigil, guarding my heart from chaos. Your strength humbles me. Can I hold the reins for a moment?

Your fear whispers of disasters you've fought alone. I'm here now, fierce and steady. Will you let me stand with you?

You've woven a shield of control through endless storms. Let love carry the weight, dear protector.

Self-Led Questions:

1.   Take three deep, settling breaths. Recall a protective part that you've noticed recently, perhaps one that plans, organizes, or worries.

2.   From a place of curiosity, ask this manager: *"What are you guarding? What truly matters to you in doing this work?"* Write down its answer, which may reveal a core value (e.g., "I value safety," "I value achievement").

3.   Now, design a "Values Banner" for your internal system. On a piece of paper or in your digital app, create a simple banner shape. Inside, write 3-5 values that resonate deeply with you (e.g., Family, Growth, Kindness, Authenticity, Purpose). You can draw simple symbols or add digital elements that represent these values.

4.   Reflect: *"How does seeing this banner of my values feel? Does it align with my manager's intention?"* E.g.: It grounds me - I find it calming, because it is aligned with my authentic self.

Creative Option: Instead of a full banner, simply list 3-5 values that come to mind.

What are my cherished Values?

MY REFLECTIONS

Day 2: Observing Thoughts with Defusion

Purpose: Detaching from the protector's thoughts using ACT Defusion.
Focus on: Thoughts from both Niggle and Skitch parts.

Try This: When you practice labeling thoughts, identify their origin. An idea like 'You're not good enough' is likely from a Niggle Part, while an urge like 'Let's just ditch this' comes from a Skitch Part. Use your custom labels in the exercise to make it more personal.

Journal's Prompt: Label it: 'My Niggling Critic is having the thought that I'll fail,' or 'My Skitchy Avoider is sending the urge to procrastinate.'

Self-to-Part Connection:

Critical Niggler says, "*You're not enough.*" You label it, accept its presence, and commit to noting one strength daily (value: self-respect).

My Thought	Part Source (Niggle, Skitch, VelFire?)	Name It (Critical, anxious, angry, concerned, diligent, fearful of rejection)	Recognize it as a thought (without acting on it)	Committed Action (Identify a values-driven action)
You will always be single, & unloved.	Harsh Niggling Critic	Fear, doubt, rejection	Thought is now on a cloud, drifting away	Take a small action to meet singles in my area

Manager's Belief Code:

'*A world built of order over overwhelm. A fortress against the memory of what happens when control is lost. A place we can never go back to.*'

Suggested Validation phrase: "*I see your tireless vigil, guarding my heart from chaos. Your strength humbles me. Can I hold the reins for a moment?*"

MY REFLECTIONS

Day 3: Noticing Your Niggle (Manager's Role)

Purpose: An exploration of a manager's role and intentions.
Focus on: A Niggle Part.
Suggestion: Treat this day as a dedicated interview with one of your most prominent manager parts. Use your specific dialogue questions to uncover its fears, its job, and what it needs to feel safer.

Journal Prompt: From Self, I will ask my *Niggling Co-Dependent*: 'I see how hard you are working. What are you worried will happen if you set boundaries? How can I help you feel safer?'

Self-to-Part Connection:

Using any method you wish, acknowledge one thing your protectors would most appreciate.

Conscious Connection with My Niggle Part

Somatic Expression of Part **(Body)**	Fears, Role, Intentions, Worries? **(Mind)**	How can *Self* bring perspective, rest & restoration? **(Self-Leadership)**	Ask: *What do you need me to acknowledge about this situation?* **(Connection)**	Act: Based on your values, take a committed action that will enhance your life. **(Committed Action)**
Neck pain	I will be punished if I don't give in	Noticing the relationship with calm & curiosity	Reciprocal giving & relating	Plan an activity that is aligned with authentic self

DAILY REFLECTIONS

Day 4: Grounding in the Present

Purpose: Using the five senses to anchor in the present and counter a Manager's urgency
Focus on: A Niggle Part
Suggestion: Recognize that the "I MUST" urgency mentioned in the journal is the classic energy of a Niggle Part pulling you into future worry. Use the Five Senses Check-In as a direct, calming antidote to that persistent "niggling" feeling.

Journal Prompt: When I notice a 'Niggle Part' thought like 'You have to get this perfect now!' I will use that as my cue to start the five senses grounding exercise.

Five Senses Check-In

1. **Ground in Self:** Pause, take a deep breath. Notice a manager thought (e.g., "I must do more") and bodily sensations (e.g., tight chest).

 ⇒ 5 things you see (e.g., pen, sunlight)
 ⇒ 4 things you hear (e.g., breath, birds)
 ⇒ 3 things you touch (e.g., chair, fabric)
 ⇒ 2 things you smell (e.g., coffee, air)
 ⇒ 1 thing you taste (e.g., saliva)

2. **Reflect on Managers:** "What did my manager say? How do I feel staying present?"
3. **Connect with Self:** Offer one kind word to the Manager or Exile (e.g., "safe").

Base of the U (Abide): Pause, bring Self presence to the part.

Empathy & Acceptance

1. IFS Empathy: From Self, say, "I see you trying to protect me." Notice its response.
2. ACT Acceptance: Accept the Manager's urgency. Say, "I'm willing to feel this to honor my value of presence."
3. Reflect: "What's this Manager protecting? What value (e.g., calm) guides me?"

ACT Action: Choose one small, values-aligned action (e.g., pause for a 1-minute sense check before reacting).

Reflect: "What's one step to honor this Manager and my values?"

U-Model™ Connection

-Descent: IFS awareness + ACT presence anchors you in the moment
-Abide (bottom of U):   IFS empathy   + ACT acceptance fosters connection
-Ascend: IFS integration + ACT action aligns with values

DAILY REFLECTIONS

Day 5: Meeting Your Self

Purpose: Connecting with your calm Leader Self
Focus on: The Self's relationship to both "Skitch" and "Niggle" parts
Suggestion: Connect with the qualities of Self (the '8 C's: Calm, Curiosity, Compassion, Confidence, Courage, Clarity, Creativity, Connectedness (9th C: *Choice*)

The Creed (or Presence) of the Self

The Self is the core of who you are - your calm, compassionate center. *It's not a part*; it's the essence of you that leads and heals the parts.

Self is the Key for the Inner Family

Its creed is a warm, steady voice from your center:

I am here.

I have always been here, and nothing can destroy me.

I am not afraid of any part of you.

All of you are welcome in my presence.

I am the calm in the storm and the light in the darkness. I meet your pain with strength and loyalty,

and your fear with steady presence.

I see your story with awareness

and hold your confusion with clarity.

We are connected.

I am whole, and I lead with Love.

Our relationship is your safe home.

It is here you most belong,

And are warmly welcome.

Self-Leadership Qualities (The 8 Cs of Self-Energy)

The Self has inherent qualities. In IFS, they are referred to as the "8 C's". They indicate you are in *Self*.

1. **Calm:** Awareness, tranquility and balance
2. **Curiosity:** An interest in understanding parts without judgment
3. **Clarity:** The ability to see situations clearly, without distortion from emotional burdens
4. **Compassion:** A caring, non-judgmental approach toward parts
5. **Confidence:** The belief in one's capacities
6. **Courage:** The choice to take values-led action in the presence of complex emotions
7. **Connectedness:** An empathic presence
8. **Creativity:** The flow of inspiration, intuition and open-mindedness

When you access the Self, you experience these qualities. This provides the healing co-regulation well-suited for your parts.

Notice when you are in a space of Self-Energy.

ASK:

How can Self lead your "Niggle Parts" with more patience and your "Skitch Parts" with more wisdom?

How can Self shift the burdened beliefs of the VelFire parts?

26

MY REFLECTIONS

Day 6: Meeting Your Firefighter (Reactive Protectors)

Purpose: Understanding the role of an impulsive Firefighter part
Focus on: A 'Skitch' Part
Suggestion: This day is a formal introduction to the Firefighter, one of your leading "Skitch Parts." When the journal asks you to recall an urge to escape or distract, identify the "Skitch" responsible and use your creative idea to sketch it. Describe its quick, fleeting energy.

Sensory Option: What sound does your Skitch Part make? Hum or describe it (e.g., *a buzzing bee for my Restless Adventurer*).

The Firefighter's Creed - An Emergency Alarm:

Firefighters are reactive protectors. They emerge *because of* an activated wounded part. Their sole purpose is to immediately extinguish the painful feeling, without regard for the consequences. By viewing their operating instructions as a "creed," you acknowledge that these parts have a purpose and a deeply held belief system. This is a key step in understanding and healing.

"Pain! Desperation is born in the chronic inferno! The alarm is sounding! Extinguish it NOW. Use any means necessary - numb it, distract from it, drown it out. The consequences don't matter; only stopping this feeling does. Escape and Survival at all costs!"

Core Beliefs:
1. The Firefighter must extinguish the emotional pain because it is intolerable and dangerous
2. Immediate relief is the only priority
3. The future doesn't matter when the present hurts this much
4. Any escape is a good escape

Here are some Self-led validating statements for your firefighter:
1. You blaze into battle to smother my pain, my selfless warrior. I'm here, unburned, ready to face the fire with you.
2. In your wild rush to save me, I feel your desperate heart. I'm not leaving you in this inferno. Can we pause together?
3. You dive into chaos to keep my wounds at bay. I see your courage. Will you trust my light to soothe the flames?

MY REFLECTIONS

Day 7: Pausing and Defusing Firefighter's Urges

Purpose: Using defusion to create space from intense Firefighter urges

Focus on: A "Skitch Part"

Suggestion: The fleeting, intense nature of Firefighter urges is the essence of a "skitch." The exercise of naming an urge as a "cloud" is perfect for this. When you feel a "skitch," give it a playful name like "*the Buy It Now cloud*" or "*the Yell cloud*" to create distance before you act.

Journal Prompt: I'll playfully name the urge: '*Ah, there's that Dissociated Skitch floating by. I see it. Alongside it is the Rough Rager. Noted.*'

Get creative and write your own!

Skitch-Defusion Technique: Write one sentence about the urge (e.g., urge to yell) or record a voice memo saying the defusion phrase.

- *A part of my mind is telling me* (fill in).
- I am not my part, and this part isn't me.
- Notice and Name: *I pause and observe any emotion or firefighter urges before acting. I notice the effect this naming has on my system.*

MY REFLECTIONS

Day 8: Firefighter's Protective Intentions

Purpose: Understanding the positive intention behind a Firefighter's impulsive actions
Focus on: A "Skitch Part"

Suggestion: The "Thank-You Note" exercise is a powerful way to connect with a "Skitch Part." Address the note to a specific skitch (e.g., *Dear Impulsive Spark*) and thank it for what it's trying to protect you from (e.g., *Thank you for trying to save me from feeling bored and trapped*).

Journal Prompt: I'll write a Thank-You Note: '*Dear Skitchy Distractor, thank you for trying to protect me from feeling overwhelmed. I appreciate your effort to keep me safe.*'

U-Model™ Exercise: Thank-You Note (IFS + ACT)

Descend: Awareness

1. Ground in Self: Take three deep breaths. Recall a firefighter's impulsive urge (e.g., procrastinate, withdraw).
-ACT Defusion: Label it: "*I notice an urge to [action].*"

2. Ask from Self: "*What pain are you shielding me from?*" Write its answer (e.g., "I block rejection").

3. Write a Thank-You Note: Address the firefighter (e.g., "*Dear Escaper*"), thank them for their protective intent (e.g., "Thank you for your intention to shield me from being flooded emotionally").

4. Reflect: "How do I feel about this firefighter now? Did this shift my view?"

Self-to-Part Connection:

- Reflect on an impulsive habit. What is the context/pattern it occurs, its form and function? What avoidance pattern might it be serving?
- List three ways the firefighter helps, or record a voice memo thanking them
- How can you bring Self-Leadership to this part today?

Example: Skitchy Escaper says, "I block rejection." You thank it, accept its urge, and commit to a brief pause before fleeing (value of courage).

MY REFLECTIONS

Day 9: Grounding with Firefighters

Purpose: Using body awareness to stay present during Firefighter activation
Focus on: A "Skitch Part"
Suggestion: A "skitch" often manifests as a physical jolt of energy. Use the Body Scan exercise to notice where that "skitchy" feeling (restlessness, frantic energy, tightness) shows up in your body. Observe it without getting carried away.

Journal Prompt: "Where in my body do I feel this 'skitch'? Is it a buzzing in my head? A tapping in my foot?"

Self-to-Part Connection:

Concentrate on a specific body part (for example, feet) for one minute or record a voice memo describing observed sensations. Example: An urge to rush is recognized. A brief somatic scan reveals chest tightness, followed by a deep, grounding breath.

"Currently, I notice, and name urges and physical sensations. I inquire what this part(s) might need from Self."

MY REFLECTIONS

Day 10: The Descent

Purpose: Reviewing the protector parts (Managers and Firefighters), you have met
Focus on: Your whole cast of "Skitch" and "Niggle" parts

Suggestion: As you review the past nine days, create two lists in your notebook: "My Niggle Parts" (the Managers you've met) and "My Skitch Parts" (the Firefighters you've met). Reflect on the different energies they bring and how your feelings toward them may have shifted.

Journal Prompt: My 'Skitch' Parts: The Distractor, The Snapper, The Impulsive Spark. What have I learned about them?"

The Situation	My "Niggle Parts" (Managers I met)	My "Skitch Parts" (Firefighters I met).	What have they revealed to me about their roles/fears/yearnings?	How does Self have a healing effect?
I shut down around people who rudely interrupt me	Fawning behavior, people-pleasing, to avoid my anger	Defend myself, confront, ignore, avoid	They have opposite ways of reacting to the uncomfortable experience	A warm, glow of a kind teacher. A calming love. Take a values-based committed action.

The Protectors' creed would sound something like:
"Never again. We must control everything to prevent that pain from surfacing. Stay vigilant, be perfect, and don't show any vulnerability. Safety comes from being prepared and staying one step ahead of any threat."

Core Beliefs:
1. Control is safety.
2. Vulnerability is dangerous.
3. Perfection prevents criticism and pain.
4. Logic must override emotion.

How do I feel towards these parts now? (Record a voice note memo about your feelings towards them, if it helps.)

MY REFLECTIONS

Day 11: Meeting Your Exile

Purpose: Gently contacting a vulnerable, wounded Exile part (*VelFire*)
Focus on: How your "Skitch" and "Niggle" parts protect the Exile
Suggestion: As you approach an Exile and its painful feeling (e.g., inadequacy), also notice which protectors get activated. Does a "Niggle Part" jump in to try to analyze or fix the feeling? Does a "Skitch Part" show up with an urge to numb it or run away?

The Exile's Creed (or Plea)
Exiles are young, tender, vulnerable parts carrying past injuries, pain, shame, and inadequacies. Their relational wounds remain frozen in time. Their beliefs echo the burdens they bear.

Recall the Exile's Creed from Part I: '*I am the one who is not okay…*' How does this resonate with your VelFire Part today?

Core Beliefs (Burdens):
1. I am fundamentally flawed/bad
2. I am unworthy of love and belonging
3. My feelings are dangerous and overwhelming
4. If people truly see me, they will reject me
5. My only hope is for someone to come and rescue me
6. To be loved, I must disappear into hiding, and have no voice or needs

A goal of IFS therapy is to approach this Exile with the compassion of the core Self, and to help them unburden their painful beliefs. While the parts' creeds are born from reaction and survival, the creed of the Self is a statement of its inherent, undamaged nature. It's not a set of rules to follow but a description of its constant, healing presence.

Here are some sample Self-led statements to use as a guided meditation, journaling prompt, or in any way that resonates with your system.

1. You've carried this aching loneliness in the dark too long. I'm kneeling beside you now, vowing you're not alone.
2. Your hidden story trembles in my heart. Speak, sweet one. I'm listening with every fiber, believing every word.
3. I believe you.
4. You belong, are welcome and cherished. No longer an exile; precious member of this family. I am here. Welcome home.

Sandcastle Storytelling

Gather some colorful toys like buckets, shovels, and small figures. In a sandbox or a tray of sand, build a sandcastle. As you create, using the toys, let your inner child take over - add towers, moats, and secret tunnels. Then, invent a fun story about the castle. Give each toy a character role - for example, a brave knight bucket or a magical shovel wizard. Speak or write the story aloud, embracing the silliness and creativity. Combining tactile play with imaginative freedom is perfect for reconnecting with your inner child!

MY REFLECTIONS

Day 12: Listening to Your (*VelFire*) Exile ('Felt Sensing')

Purpose: Deepening your connection by compassionately listening to an Exile
Focus on: Asking your "Skitch" and "Niggle" parts for space
Suggestion: Before writing the compassionate letter to your Exile, as the exercise suggests, add a preliminary step from your own framework. Extend a kind request: *"Dear Skitch-a-Niggle, I see you and thank you for your protection. I'm asking for a little space now so Self can listen to this wounded part."*

Journal Prompt: From Self, I'll ask my protectors to soften: '*Niggling Fixer, can you please relax for a moment?*' Then, I will pause and notice what sensations and emotions are present. I will turn to the Exile and ask: '*Where do you want to go from here?*'

Committed Action: Identify a need you usually avoid due to uncomfortable emotions. Take a small values-based step toward fulfilling it. Notice how it lands with your system. Take this action, despite complex feelings that may arise (psychological flexibility).

A Felt Sensing Partnership

My VelFire's (Exile) Needs (Open)	My awareness of these needs, expressed in Felt Sensing or any other way (Aware)	Self-Led Committed Action (Engaged)
To be heard To repair ruptures lovingly To be cared for To be treated fairly	A gentle sense in my solar plexus A vision of a toddler being held by me, wrapped in a soft blanket	Spending time in safe spaces Playful, creative moments Allowing myself to be heard, cared for, and loved

41

MY REFLECTIONS

Day 13: Welcoming Exile (VelFire) Pain

Purpose: Embracing an Exile's painful emotions with radical acceptance

Focus on: The reactions of your "Skitch" and "Niggle" parts to the Exile's pain

Suggestion: As you practice welcoming an emotion like grief or shame, also welcome the reactions of the protectors. Notice the "niggle" wanting to analyze or the "skitch" to escape. Welcoming the pain means welcoming all the internal activity that comes with it, including the fear from your other parts (open, aware, and engaged).

Journal Prompt: I welcome my Exile's feelings of shame (name whatever emotions surface). I notice my 'Niggle Part' wants to understand it. And my 'Skitch Part' wants to numb it. I can be present with all three.

In this moment, I become aware of how my various parts communicate through my body. I accept exiles' emotions as meaningful messages. If grief arises, I hold it safely for healing.

MY REFLECTIONS

Day 14: Psychological Flexibility & Exploring Co-Dependency

Purpose: Identifying co-dependent parts (like a "Pleaser") and responding with flexibility
Focus on: Determining if a co-dependent part has a "skitch" or "niggle" energy
Suggestion: When mapping a part like the "Pleaser", analyze its style. Is it a "Niggle-Pleaser" that meticulously worries about and manages everyone else's feelings? Or is it a "Skitch-Pleaser" that impulsively says "yes" to avoid the immediate discomfort of saying "no"?

Journal Prompt: "I'll name this part and its energy. Is it my 'Niggling Caretaker' or my 'Skitchy Appeaser'? The strategy to help it might be different.

Reflect on a time you felt overly responsible (hardworking parts blended and fused with you). What actions did you take? With your present knowledge, what might be a value-driven alternative?

U-Model™ **Connection:**

- Descent (IFS mapping with ACT) reveals co-dependency
- Base: Pause, introduce Self presence to the part and its burden or role
- Empathy and flexibility lead to acceptance
- Ascend (integration and action) ensures alignment with values

Example: A Manager-Pleaser part is concerned about rejection. You:

- Recognize its needs,
- Respond by *pausing before agreeing* (value: coherence and self-respect),
- Become aware of co-dependent parts with observation and openness.

Committed Action: Do something for yourself that you typically extend to others, reflecting personal values. For instance, assess your need for play, fun, or restoration. What actions can you take that are consistent with your values? Can you request reciprocity where you need it?

MY REFLECTIONS

Day 15: Exploring Boundaries

Purpose: Identifying parts that are activated by their own, or others', boundary-setting

Focus on: How both 'Skitch' and 'Niggle' parts react to boundaries

Suggestion: A 'Niggle Part' might prevent you from setting a boundary by endlessly worrying about the consequences. A 'Skitch Part' might hijack you (blend/fuse with you), creating an impulse to give in immediately just to escape the awkward feeling. As you map your boundary struggle, identify which part(s) hops in the driver's seat.

Journal Prompt: My 'Niggling Worrier' fears conflict, so it paralyzes me. My 'Skitchy Avoider' also fears conflict, but its strategy is to give in immediately. Which one is more active right now?

U-Model™ Connection:

- Descent (IFS mapping and ACT presence) reveals boundary issues
- Pausing with self-awareness and empathy brings clarity
- Ascend (integration and action) helps align actions with values

Observe. Reflect. Express

This week, **observe which boundaries are the most difficult to set and in which situations**. Take a moment to reflect on personal values. Express one need as an initial step toward addressing it. Consider the practical actions you can take to address protector fears.

Examples:

- Reciprocity
- Emotional attunement
- Relational integrity and respect
- Relational repair

47

MY REFLECTIONS

Day 16: Mid-Journey Reflection

Parts Flexibility Inventory (PFI) and Self-Connection Inventory (SCI)

Purpose: Assessing progress by retaking the **PFI and SCI inventories**

Focus on: Reflecting specifically on your relationship with your "Skitch" and "Niggle" parts

Suggestion: When you review your scores, frame your reflections around your compassion for your parts. *"Have I developed more compassion for my 'Niggle Parts'? Do I feel more space and choice when a 'Skitch Part' gets activated?"*

Journal Prompt: Comparing my scores, I can appreciate the protective intent of my 'niggles,' and I can pause before acting on a 'skitch.' My *Self* can lead them both.

Reflection:

Notice how these subtle shifts - greater compassion for your 'Niggle Parts' and gentler leadership over your 'Skitch Parts' - create a foundation for **deeper internal trust**. The process of naming and understanding your internal dynamics is an act of care.

As you move forward, let curiosity guide your attention: *What new capacities for flexibility are emerging? How might you invite your parts into collaboration rather than conflict?*

Revisit your intention:

Allow all parts, even the ones carrying discomfort or urgency, to feel seen and considered. This softening opens space for compassionate dialogue, a crucial pivot. Your parts hear the voice of Self responding with care.

MY REFLECTIONS

Day 17: Compassionate Conversations

Purpose: Using Self-led dialogue to offer direct compassion to an Exile

Focus on: Visualizing your "Skitch" and "Niggle" parts as witnesses to the healing

Suggestion: As you write the dialogue between Self and an Exile, imagine your other parts are watching. The dialogue helps them learn that Self can handle the Exile's pain, allowing them to relax. You can even add a note in your journal like, "My Niggling Critic and Skitchy Distractor are observing this conversation from a safe distance, learning to trust my Self."

Journal Prompt: I'll write the dialogue between Self and the Exile. I'll imagine my 'niggles' and 'skitches' are also listening, seeing that Self can be present with the pain **without needing to fix it or flee.**

Flexible Perspective: Observe when you identify with your Exile part ('*VelFire*') and shift to an observer perspective. Reflect on the current needs of this part without becoming fully involved. Examine unworkable actions this part has proposed. **Consider how Self-Energy could be helpful in this situation**.

Committed Action: Schedule a time this week to engage in a carefree, values-based activity you've wanted to try. Somatically, did you notice any shifts in your body?

MY REFLECTIONS

Day 18: Understanding Past Hurts

Purpose: Exploring the origin story of an Exile's pain
Focus on: Connecting a past hurt to the creation of your "Skitch" and "Niggle" parts.

Suggestion: After you witness the Exile's story, add a reflection: Because of this past hurt, what job did my 'Niggle Parts' take on? (e.g., hard-working, need to control everything). What job did my 'Skitch Parts' take on? (e.g., to numb or avoid any similar feelings). The Exile's story links their protector's current roles to their origin.

Journal Prompt: After writing the Exile's story of being exiled out of my awareness, I'll reflect: *'This is when my Niggling Pleaser was born to prevent that from happening again. And when my Skitchy Avoider learned to escape situations that felt similar. A perfect match of protective avoidance.'*

Visualization for Healing

Find a Quiet Space: Sit comfortably, close your eyes, and take a few deep breaths. Imagine a safe, beautiful path (e.g., a forest trail, beach, or garden) in your mind's eye.

1.   Invite Your Hurting Part to Walk: Picture your younger, hurting part (Exile) walking beside you on this path. Offer it silent comfort, perhaps imagining holding its hand or saying, *"I'm here for you now."*

2.   Meet Your Protectors on the Path: Notice your "Niggle" (e.g., Pleaser) and "Skitch" (e.g., Avoider) parts in the scene. Are they smoothing the path or hiding nearby? Acknowledge their protective roles with curiosity and gratitude.

3.   A Values-Driven Moment: On your inner path, perform a small, symbolic action reflecting your Self's values (e.g., admire a flower for appreciation, help a creature for kindness, or stand tall for confidence).

4.   Reflect and Return: Gently end the visualization, thank your parts, and notice any shifts in your inner world. Journal your reflections, noting any sense of calm or connection you experience.

MY REFLECTIONS

Day 19: Creating Safe Spaces

Purpose: Designing a safe, healing inner sanctuary for an Exile

Focus on: Asking your 'Skitch' and 'Niggle' parts which roles they would prefer, if they did not have to work so hard (trust in Self leadership was present).

Suggestion: As you visualize the safe space, you can invite your protectors to rest. You could ask your 'Niggling Organizer' to ensure the space is secure, or you could ask your 'Skitchy Rusher' to take a nap outside, trusting that Self is safely leading.

Journal Prompt: I'm creating a warm, cozy den for my Small One. I will ask my parts to find a safe, comfortable spot to unwind. I will ask my 'Niggling Guard' to stand watch outside the door, and my 'Skitchy Distractor' to find a fun toy to bring back later. The Exile is safe inside with my *Self*.

A Warm, Safe Space

Gently create a warm haven for your Small One, whispering, "My loving Self has made this cozy space just for you!" Invite your inner team to contribute. Your Niggle adds comforting touches, and your Skitch sparks joy nearby. Then celebrate this tender collaboration, exclaiming, "My parts are learning to trust Self's care, and work together!"

MY REFLECTIONS

Day 20: Healing Through Presence

Purpose: Using non-judgmental presence to soothe and heal an Exile.

Focus on: Resisting the urge to "niggle" or "skitch" away from the present moment.

The Presence of Self: The act of being present with a painful feeling is the direct opposite of what your protectors want to do. Notice the "niggle" to nix the feeling, and the "skitch" to escape it. Your focused presence is choosing to stay with the Exile despite intense emotional signals.

Journal Prompt: As I sit with this anxiety, I feel the 'niggle' to problem-solve and the 'skitch' to check my phone. I notice and name these parts; however they make themselves known, gently returning my focus to the feeling, telling the Exile, 'I'm here with you.'

Accessible Option: Be present with any emotion for 1 min or record a voice memo saying, "I'm here."

Base of the U:

- Pause and bring awareness to the part
- Acknowledge the role of each part with curiosity
- Affirm the part(s) with empathy and acceptance

Pocket Practice: A Breath of Presence!

Gently sit with your Small One's feelings, breathing deeply and whispering, "*My loving Self is here, staying with you!*" When Niggle's urge to overthink or Skitch's pull to escape arises, anchor in a slow breath, journal the moment, and exclaim, "*My Presence of Self is healing us!*"

Is there a shift that you notice?

MY REFLECTIONS

Day 21: Leading with Self

Purpose: Practicing leading your entire inner system from a state of Self.
Focus on: Having Your *Self* mediate a conversation between your "Skitch" and "Niggle" parts.

Creative Activity: Have the *Self* lead a meeting.

From Self, I ask my Niggling Planner: 'What do you need?'
Then I ask my Skitchy Dreamer: 'What do you need?'
How can Self leadership help you both work together?

This Self-to-Part meeting is a creative way to practice integrating their dynamics.

Journal Prompt: Divide a sheet of paper into two columns. Using two different colored pens (or pencils), start a dialogue between two parts that are at odds with each other. Keep writing for your parts. If they were in your living room right now and could verbalize their conflicts, what would they say? How would they sound? What core vulnerabilities, fears, and yearnings would come to light? How would your Self lead their mediation? What would be a Self-led intervention?

Self-Mediates

From Self, guide a heart-to-heart and ask your parts what stirs them? What are their burdens? Unite them with your Self-leadership and calm wisdom. *"I see my parts at odds. From Self's steady throne, I'll pen a dialogue. As trust evolves, we will know each other. Committed action steps will become a partnership."*

PART	PART	SELF MEDIATES
Sample Parts: *Niggling Critic*	*Furious Firefighter*	
Example: Niggling Critic is highly critical, out of fear of failure. It believes that if it harshly criticizes, you won't make mistakes.	*A furious firefighter caught a shame-based Exile emerging into conscience awareness. It went from 0 to 100 to prevent system overwhelm.*	*What are your roles, fears, and burdens? Where do you both disagree (the approach, method, means, end goal)?*

59

MY REFLECTIONS

Day 22: Acting on Values

Purpose: Taking a small, committed action toward your values, acknowledging parts' objections (without obeying them)

Focus on: Identifying whether objection to action comes from a Skitch, Niggle, or VelFire part (firefighter, manager, or exile part)

Suggestion: When you choose your action, anticipate the objection. Is it a "Niggle Part" with a list of worries ("What if you fail?")? Or is it a "Skitch Part" with an impulsive counteroffer ("This is hard, let's do something fun!")? Naming the source of the objection helps you meet it with compassion

Journal Prompt: *"I would like to practice my presentation ahead of schedule. I anticipate my 'Niggling Doubter' will resist with fears of imperfection, and my 'Skitchy Avoider' will resist with the urge to clean the house instead."*

U-Model™ Connection: Descent (identify objections with IFS), Empathy (accept parts' resistance), Ascent (act on values with Self-leadership).

Committed Action: Plan a small values-driven action for tomorrow - notice and name which parts are activated. Bring Self-Energy to those parts.

MY REFLECTIONS

Day 23: Harmonizing Parts

Purpose: Visualizing your dominant parts working together harmoniously.
Focus on: A Skitch and Niggle Part in a cooperative relationship

Suggestion: This is the perfect day to use your *Sketch Your Parts* ideas. Draw or describe a scene where a Niggle Part and a Skitch Part are working together under Self's leadership. For example, the Niggling Planner builds a safe bridge, and the Skitchy Adventurer joyfully runs across it.

Journal Prompt: I will sketch a scene: My Niggling Planner is like a gardener tending the soil, and my Skitchy Creative part is like a bee, pollinating the flowers. Both are needed for the garden to thrive.

Committed Action: First, my Niggling Planner (Gardener) created a practical Sunday schedule by outlining essential chores and errands. Then, my Skitchy Creative (Bee) pollinated this structure by infusing it with joyful details. We explored a nature trail instead of exercising indoors and added a spontaneous trip to a local artsy café afterwards.

MY REFLECTIONS

Day 24: Defusing Obstacles

Purpose: Using defusion to lessen the power of thoughts that block your Self.

Focus on: Labeling obstacle thoughts as "Skitch Clouds", "Niggle Clouds", or "VelFire Clouds".

Suggestion: When an obstacle thought arises, identify its energy. A persistent, heavy thought like "*This will never work*" might be a "Niggle Cloud." A sudden, distracting thought, like "*I'm too tired for this,*" might be a "Skitch Cloud." Using your labels makes the defusion technique more personal.

Journal Prompt: "I'm noticing a 'niggling' thought that 'I'm going to mess this up.' I will visualize it as a slow, heavy, Gray 'Niggle Cloud' and watch it drift by."

Committed Action: Catch a thought. See it as a thought, not a fact. What shifts?

If it is a 'barrier-thought' (consistently gets in your way), defuse it. Then, pivot immediately to a small, values-driven action.

If the Thought Is	And You Value	Your Action Could Be
I'm not good enough	Growth	Read one page of a book that mirrors your true Self
I'm too anxious to go	Community	RSVP to the event
This project is too big	Diligence	Open the document. Write one sentence.

MY REFLECTIONS

Day 25: The Three Voices

Purpose: Strengthening the Self's capacity to be with discomfort gracefully.

Focus on: Showing your Skitch and Niggle parts that Self can handle discomfort.

Suggestion: Flexibility is the ability of Self to stay present when your Niggle Parts urge to fix and your Skitch Parts plan to flee. As you practice the anchoring exercise, you are actively demonstrating to your whole system that Self can handle it.

Journal Prompt: *"As I allow myself to feel this discomfort of waiting for an answer, I notice the 'niggle' to recheck my email and the 'skitch' to distract myself. I'll anchor myself by feeling my feet on the floor, letting my Self hold the discomfort for them."*

Creative Option: Write one psychologically flexible moment or record a voice memo saying, *"I accept my inner world, am present, and engaged with my values."*

Committed Action: What does your system need from Self today? Meet that need with awareness of how your system responds. Keep a tracking log of these experiences (fulfilling your system's yearnings in small, measurable ways). Checking in with your system is the opposite of avoidance and is the royal road to a more fulfilling life.

The Three Voices Chart: A comprehensive daily record

1. Tracks events
2. Explores the underlying dialogue and needs of your internal system
3. Creating a clear path from parts-activation to values-led action (*'Self can hold this feeling'*)

Date/ Time	The Discomfort/Part Activation	My 'Niggle' Urge (To Fix/ Control)	My 'Skitch' Urge (To Flee/Avoid)	My Self (The Anchor)	How My System Responded
January 2	Waiting for an important email.	Compulsive reliance on external activities	Let's just watch a show or scroll through social media to forget about it.	Took three deep breaths. Felt my feet planted firmly on the floor. "Self can hold this feeling of uncertainty."	The urgency faded. Felt a sense of calm and capability. The compulsion to check email lessened.

MY REFLECTIONS

Day 26: Committing to Action

Today, you'll make a firm commitment to live out one of your core values. The challenge? Acknowledge the complex emotions that surround taking necessary and committed action.

Know Your Self-Energy

To stay on track, you will need Self-Energy.

- Niggles: Persistent, rationalizing thoughts that argue against your commitment. They sound convincing (e.g., *"You need to finish one more task first!"*).
- Skitches: Restless, impulsive urges craving instant gratification (e.g., *"Just scroll for five more minutes!"*).
- VelFire: Beliefs of being unworthy, prone to being a failure, or rejected.

Naming these forces before they strike strips away their power. Extending them curious compassion, a felt presence, and connection will help them develop trust in your leadership.

Your Commitment Practice

Name your commitment in two parts: the action tied to your value and the objection you expect. Naming your niggles, skitches, and velfire burdens upfront, you are ready to address them. This frees you up to choose your values over distractions.

Example 1: Meditation

Commitment: "I'll meditate for 5 minutes to honor my value of Calm."
    Resistance: "My Niggling Planner will say it's a waste of time, and my Skitchy Distractor will push me to check my phone."

Example 2: Screen Time

Commitment: "I'll shut off screens by 10 PM for my value of Rest."
    Resistance: "My Niggling Worker will insist I check one more email, and my Skitchy Binger will beg to finish the next episode."
Write your commitment now. Name your value, specify your action, and notice how parts are reacting. Acknowledge them, then recommit to your action. Choose your values whilst acknowledging your impulses (parts reactivity). What happens when you take the committed action, despite parts reactivity?

For example, your value might be teaching. Some of your parts are fearful that you do not appear knowledgeable or will blunder the communication. You take action to learn, practice and receive coaching on public speaking. You start small and teach a small group of people. You learn and grow in teaching, through practice, engagement, and integrating constructive feedback.

MY REFLECTIONS

Day 27: Celebrating Progress

Purpose:　　　　Acknowledging and celebrating the growth your parts have made.

Focus on:　　　　An honorable mention to the parts who came forward. Maybe it is their first time speaking up, and/or feeling heard.

Suggestion:　　　　Direct your celebration toward your parts. *I want to celebrate the moment my 'Niggling Critic' offered a gentle suggestion instead of a harsh judgment. I want to celebrate my 'Skitchy Avoider' for allowing us to stay in a difficult conversation for one minute longer. Thank you both for your progress.*

Journal Prompt:　　Yesterday, I felt an impulse from my 'Skitchy Spender' during a difficult, emotional conversation. I was able to pause, notice, and name the feelings, connect them somatically, and act based on my values. That's a huge win for my *Self* and for that part.

Creative Option:　　List one recent values-based move, where typically, your protectors might draw you to avoidance-based actions (fear). Your Self led the way this time!

U-Model™ Connection:

Descent (IFS reflection + ACT presence) supports growth; pausing with Self-awareness allows empathy and acceptance, building gratitude.

Ascend (integration + action) aligns actions with values.

Committed Action: What does your system need from your Self today? Can you act on it by applying your values?

Write it down, set a date, time and a measurable description, sharing with an accountability partner. When completed, return to this entry, and describe its completion.

Example: *Every Monday, starting this Monday, I will walk in nature for thirty minutes.*

MY REFLECTIONS

Day 28: Integrating Values and Parts

Purpose: Aligning the energy of your parts with your core values for a more harmonious system

Focus on: Giving your Skitch and Niggle parts new, positive, values-aligned jobs

Suggestion: This is a key integration day

Ask a Niggle Part: How can your talent for analysis support my value of Wisdom?

Ask a Skitch Part: How can your quick energy support my value of Playfulness?

Values alignment helps transform their roles from unseen to collaborative, authentic, and unburdened.

Committed Action: What values-based action will move your life forward at this time?

Helpful Tips

- Notice when parts are distracting you away from your committed actions
- Lovingly attune to them, inquire about their protective concerns, and remember that you **do not** have any bad parts

MY REFLECTIONS

Day 29: Facing Future Challenges

Purpose: Creating a Self-led plan to navigate future challenges with your parts

Focus on: How Self will lead your Skitch, Niggle, and VelFire parts

Suggestion: When you identify a future challenge, create a step-by-step plan for your parts. *"When the challenge begins, I will acknowledge the fear from my Niggling Worrier and thank it. I will take three deep breaths to calm my Skitchy Reactor. I will then let my Self speak, guided by my value of courage."*

Journal Prompt: My Self-led plan for the upcoming family dinner: *"When my Niggling Critic starts judging, I will offer it compassion. When my Skitchy Defender wants to make a sharp comment, I will pause and lead with my value of peace."*

Creative Option: Check in with your internal family often. What do they need? Write one core yearning that you are open and aware of. Allow Self to lead the way!

Essential Question: How did that work out for you?

MY REFLECTIONS

Day 30: Committing to Your Journey

A heartfelt commitment to your ongoing path of Self-leadership

The Self-Energized Leader

I promise to explore further the family of parts within.
I will continue to listen to my Niggle Parts' concerns
and honoring my Skitch Parts energy
I will guide my 'Skitch-a-Niggle' system from my peaceful, loving Self
I will show kindness to my VelFire parts, attending to their pain, emotions, and needs like a loving parent
And when I don't, I'll do a U-turn and find my way back to the parts of myself,
in compassion, curiosity, and connection
All my parts are welcome and belong in this family system
Although my parts are not as I, or I, not them, I appreciate and am grateful for their protective, dedicated
role in my life
I wouldn't be where I am now without them
Today is the day I GET to be my team's trusty leader
And rest in my care, maybe for the first time
A new relationship is forming here; notice, aware, values-engaged,
It is an energy of calmness, clarity, curiosity, compassion, confidence, courage, creativity,
connectedness, and making choices from flexible awareness.

Journal Prompt: I, [Name], commit to my ongoing Self-to-Part Dialogue, checking in with curiosity and kindness, for my core value of growth.

Creative Option: Write a Self-led growth goal, based on the previous twenty-nine days of creative journaling.

Final Reflection

How have these thirty days of IFS-ACT journaling affected your experience? What shifts do you notice? Perhaps there is more space inside, an increased sense of safety, community and belonging. A true coming home to your body. Maybe for the first time. Welcome home to your *Self*, dear reader. I hope taking this dedicated thirty-day journey was helpful and reached parts of your mind not previously connected with. This is the power and presence of **Self-to-part connection**. While it is not necessary nor possible to know every part of your mind, your Self leadership creates safety for them all.

MY REFLECTIONS

Celebration Ritual

Thank your *Self* for leading this journey. Keep it in your wallet as a reminder of your growth.

Part III: Reflecting and Moving Forward

Surveying Your Internal Family System

Congratulations on completing your 30-day journey into your inner internal family system! Completing this exploration is a profound achievement. Now, take a moment to reflect on the transformation that has occurred within your inner circle. By engaging with your protector parts (managers and firefighters), offering empathy, respect, and kindness to your exiles, you step into the role of their leader (Self-leadership). You choose to create a deeper understanding, harmony, and purpose within.

Let's take a final look at your progress with the **Parts Flexibility Inventory (PFI) and Self-Connection Inventory (SCI).**

Exercise: Final Review (15 minutes)

Materials: Your tracking table (below), paper, or a digital app.

Self-Led Questions:

1. Find a quiet space and take a few moments to appreciate yourself for this dedicated journey.

2. Complete the **Parts Flexibility Inventory (PFI)** and the **Self-Connection Inventory (SCI)** for Day 30.

3. Go to the Tracking Table below and record your Day 30 scores.

4. Now, compare your scores from Day 1, Day 16, and Day 30. Notice any changes, big or small.

5. Write down your reflections: "What significant changes do I see in my scores, or in my overall experience of my parts and my Self? Which parts feel more flexible, less burdened, or more aligned? How has my Self-connection deepened?"

6. Finally, set a realistic, values-aligned goal for your continued journey (e.g., "I will practice pausing when my firefighters urge me to react for the next week," or "I will spend 10 minutes each morning connecting with my Self").

Accessible Option: Write down just one key insight or positive change you noticed during the journey. Or record a voice memo summarizing your experience.

Parts Flexibility Inventory (PFI)

The PFI is a 12-item measure of your flexibility in relation to your parts - Managers, Firefighters, and Exiles.

- There are four questions for each type, and for each question, the score ranges from 1 (Strongly Disagree) to 5 (Strongly Agree), resulting in a total score of 4-20 per type and 12-60 across all three types.
- The more you score, the greater your flexibility becomes in witnessing and participating with your parts, rather than being dominated by them. Low scores indicate potential areas for development.
- Fill in the PFI on Days 1, 16, and 30, and record your scores in the table at the bottom.

PFI Questions: Please indicate the extent to which you agree or disagree with the statements by rating them from 1 (Strongly Disagree) to 5 (Strongly Agree).

Managers (Proactive protectors focused on control and safety)
1. I can recognize my controlling thoughts as just thoughts, not commands.
2. I can appreciate the protective intent behind my perfectionistic tendencies.
3. I can act with self-compassion when I feel internal pressure.
4. I feel confident in my abilities, even when a part of me fears failure.

Firefighters (Reactive protectors driven by impulse to numb pain)
5. I can pause before acting on an impulse like anger or craving.
6. I can stay present with discomfort without needing to escape it.
7. I can approach my reactive impulses with kindness and curiosity
8. I can find a sense of calm within me during an emotional storm.

Exiles (Young, vulnerable parts holding pain and trauma)
9. I feel compassion toward the most hurt parts of myself.
10. I can listen to my painful emotions without judging them.
11. I am curious about my past experiences and inner world.
12. I feel hopeful that my wounded parts can heal over time.

Self-Connection Inventory (SCI)

The SCI is a five-item tool that assesses your connection to your Self -the calm, compassionate center that guides your internal system.

Each question can be rated from 1 (Strongly Disagree) to 5 (Strongly Agree) with a possible total score = 5-25.

Higher scores indicate stronger Self-leadership.

Fill out the SCI on Days 1, 16, and 30 and record your scores in the table.

SCI Questions: Please rate each item from 1 (Strongly Disagree) to 5 (Strongly Agree).

1. I feel calm when I observe my internal parts without judgment.
2. I approach my parts with curiosity and compassion
3. I can stay present with my parts even during difficult moments.
4. I trust my ability to lead my parts with confidence and clarity.
5. I make conscious choices to foster connection and creativity within my inner system.

Scoring and Tracking

Fill in both inventories on Day 1, Day 16 (a reflection halfway through your journey), and Day 30 (your final review), with the questions above.

Keep track of your tallies in the tracking table provided at the bottom. You can use a pencil or keep score in a digital app for convenience.

After every inventory, ponder in your dedicated journal: "What do my scores tell me about my relationship with my parts and my Self today?" Stronger scores pertain to Flexibility (PFI) and Self-Connection (SCI), and every score is helpful.

Approach your results with non-judgmental curiosity, as they are all part of your healing path to recovery.

Table Tracking

Parts Flexibility Inventory (PFI) and Self-Connection Inventory (SCI)

Use this table to score your PFI and SCI on Days 1, 16, and 30. These are baseline insights about your internal system. The higher the scores, the more flexibility you have with parts, and the greater Self-connection - though all scores contain information about your development. After each entry, ask yourself: *"What are my scores telling me about my relationship to my parts and my Self today?"*

DAY	MANAGERS	FIREFIGHTERS	EXILES	SELF-CONNECTION
1	4-20	4-20	4-20	5-25
16	4-20	4-20	4-20	5-25
30	4-20	4-20	4-20	5-25

Example: Day 1 Managers Score: 12 (3+3+3+3). *I noticed I struggle to see controlling thoughts as just thoughts, so I'll focus on defusion exercises.*

Reflection: What's one thing I learned about my parts or Self today? Even a 1-point increase shows growth-celebrate it!

Continuing Your Journey

Your 30-day journey is a powerful beginning, *not an end*. Here are some ways to continue your path of self-discovery and Self-leadership:

- Revisit Favorite Days: Go back to any day in Part II that resonated deeply, or where you felt a significant breakthrough. Repetition builds mastery.
- Weekly Check-In: Set aside 10 minutes each Sunday to ask, 'How is my Self leading my parts this week?' Use a favorite prompt from Part II.

- Try Optional Explorations: Dive into the additional exercises provided in Chapter 2 of this section to deepen specific areas of your practice.
- Explore Resources: utilize the glossary and additional resources in Chapter 3 to learn more, find support, and connect with IFS and ACT communities.

Optional Explorations

These exercises offer opportunities to deepen your practice and explore different facets of your inner world:

Safe Space Visualization (15 minutes)

Purpose: To create a safe space for any part that needs refuge.

Instructions: Close your eyes and imagine a place that feels completely safe, nurturing, and peaceful. Engage all your senses: What do you see, hear, smell, touch, and even taste in this space? Describe it in detail or draw it. Invite any part that needs comfort or safety to reside there.

Accessible Option: Write a detailed description of your ideal safe space. Or record a voice memo guiding yourself through the visualization.

Part Dialogue Script (15 minutes)

Purpose: To practice conscious, written dialogue between your Self and a specific part (especially a wounded part or a challenging protector).

Instructions: Choose one part you want to communicate with. Write a script, clearly labeling who is speaking (e.g., "Self:", "Part Name:"). Start with your Self's compassionate curiosity, listen to the part's response, and respond with understanding and reassurance. Aim for authentic, non-judgmental dialogue.

Accessible Option: List three questions your *Self* want to ask a part, and three things that part might need to tell your *Self*. Or record a voice memo speaking both sides of a brief dialogue.

Values Vision Board (15 minutes)

Purpose: To visually represent your core values and inspire committed action.

Instructions: Gather old magazines, print images, or use a digital collage app (e.g., Pinterest). Find pictures, words, or symbols that represent your core values (e.g., nature for connection, books for growth, hands for kindness). Arrange them on a board or digital canvas. Place it somewhere visible as a daily reminder.

Accessible Option: List three value-based goals you want to achieve in the next month. Or record a voice memo explaining why specific images or words represent your values.

Glossary

Acceptance: Welcoming thoughts, feelings, and sensations without trying to change or fight them.

ACT (Acceptance and Commitment Therapy): A therapeutic approach that helps individuals live a rich, complete, and meaningful life by accepting what is out of their personal control and committing to action that enriches life.

Ascent (*U-Model™*): The final phase of the journey, where Self leads parts in taking committed action aligned with values.

Blending: When a part's feelings, thoughts, or urges become so intense that you feel overwhelmed or consumed by them, making it challenging to access Self-Energy (e.g., feeling completely consumed by fear).

Committed Action: Taking values-based action, even when experiencing complex thoughts or feelings.

Defusion: A skill of stepping back from thoughts and seeing them as just words or mental events, rather than believing them as absolute truths.

Descent (*U-Model™*): The initial phase of the journey, focusing on meeting and understanding protector and exile parts (Managers, Firefighters, and Exiles).

Empathy: Self offers compassionate resonance.

Exiles: Parts formed during childhood or moments of intense vulnerability. The young, vulnerable parts hold the burdens of pain, shame, fear, and trauma. The rest of the internal system forces them into hiding to protect the person from their overwhelming emotions and to prevent further harm. These parts are desperately in need of being seen, heard, and healed.

Felt Sensing: (Used interchangeably with Focusing). Paying attention to a specific kind of vague, fuzzy, or unclear internal sensation that carries an implicit sense of a situation, problem, or aspect of your life.

Firefighter: An IFS "Firefighter" part. These parts react quickly and often impulsively to douse emotional pain or distress that has already arisen (e.g., through distractions, addictions, numbness, or anger).

Focusing: The structured, step-by-step process of turning your attention inward to find and stay with a felt sense. Developed by Eugene Gendlin, it's a therapeutic method that helps you approach this vague bodily sensation gently, hold it with curiosity, and allow its inherent meaning, words, or images to emerge. When the meaning fully appears, it often brings a feeling of relief or release, known as a "felt shift." **Felt Sensing is the experience**, and **Focusing is the practice** of intentionally engaging with that experience to gain insight and promote personal growth and change.

IFS (Internal Family Systems): A comprehensive, powerfully transformative, evidence-based model of psychotherapy that views the mind as naturally multiple, made up of various sub-personalities or "parts," all led by an essential core Self.

Manager: An IFS "Manager" part. These parts are proactive, often planning, controlling, or organizing to keep the system safe and avoid perceived dangers or pain.

Parts: The various sub-personalities within the mind, each with its own beliefs, feelings, and roles.

Presence: Being fully aware and engaged in the current moment.

Protectors: A general term for managers and firefighters. Parts that work to protect the system from pain or perceived threats.

Self-Energy: The state of mind associated with being in Self, characterized by the 8 Cs.

Self: The essence of who you are, characterized by qualities like: Curiosity, Calm, Compassion, Confidence, Courage, Clarity, Connectedness, and Creativity - the natural leader of the internal system.

U-Model™: The overarching framework for this journey, combining ACT and IFS therapy. It is a cyclical path of Descent (meeting protectors), Empathy (healing wounded parts), and Ascent (leading with Self and values).

Values: What truly matters to you and enriches your life in a meaningful way.

Bibliography

Adult Children of Alcoholics World Service Organization. (2012). *Adult children of alcoholics/dysfunctional families: Big red book*. Adult Children of Alcoholics World Service Organization. ISBN 978-0-9789797-8-2

Adult Children of Alcoholics World Service Organization. (2018). *The loving parent guidebook: The solution is to become your own loving parent*. Adult Children of Alcoholics World Service Organization. ISBN 978-0-9789797-5-1

Anderson, F., Schwartz, R. C., & Sweezy, M. (2017*). Internal Family Systems skills training manual: Trauma-informed treatment for anxiety, depression, PTSD & substance abuse*.

Cornell, A. W., & McGavin, B. (2005). *The radical acceptance of everything: Living a focused life*. Calluna Press.

Culver, R. (2022). The survive/thrive spiral: Trauma: IFS & the nervous system [Infographic]. Calm Heart. https://www.calmheart.co.uk

Harris, R. (2019). *ACT made simple: An easy-to-read primer on acceptance and commitment therapy* (2nd ed.). New Harbinger Publications.

Hayes, S. C. (2019). *A liberated mind: How to pivot toward what matters*. Avery.

Hayes, S. C., & Smith, S. (2005). *Get out of your mind and into your life: The new acceptance and commitment therapy*. New Harbinger Publications.

Hayes, S. C., Strosahl, K. D., & Wilson, K. G. (2012). *Acceptance and Commitment Therapy: The process and practice of mindful change* (2nd ed.). Guilford Press.

Schwartz, R. C., & Sweezy, M. (2023). *Internal Family Systems Therapy* (2nd ed.). Guilford Press.

Sweezy, M., & Ziskind, E. L. (2013). *Internal Family Systems Therapy: New Dimensions*. Routledge

Resources

Apps for Mindfulness & Self-Compassion:

Insight Timer: For a wide variety of guided meditations, including IFS and ACT-informed practices.

Calm or Headspace: General meditation apps that can support presence and acceptance.

Websites

ifs-institute.com The official website for the IFS Institute, offering training, resources, and a directory of providers.

https://contextualscience.org/ The official website for the Association for Contextual Behavioral Science (ACBS), offering training, resources, and a directory of providers.

Finding a therapist

This journal is not a substitute for therapy. If you are experiencing significant distress, please seek professional support.

U-Model™ Reference

Refer to this diagram to guide your ongoing journey. Download a printable version at www.rivkaedery.com.

Acknowledgements

From the bottom of my heart, I thank my Higher Power for providing me with *The U Model™: ACT & IFS*. It has been a guiding light in the composition of *Between Self and Parts: A 30-Day Journey of Self-Discovery with ACT & IFS*.

Your constant support-my teachers, mentors, friends, and family members-has helped weave this book into a web of warmth and grace.

This work would not be possible without the brilliant, innovative, compassionate leadership of these visionary scientists:

Dr. Richard Schwartz, founder of *Internal Family Systems Therapy* (IFS). Your Internal Family Systems model has shown us that within each human being is an ecosystem of "parts," and our authentic essence is boundless compassion. Moreover, by providing a vocabulary for understanding my inner world and a way to allow its own healing, your work has transformed my life. Thank you so much for what you've given as a visionary scientist, healer, and visionary thinker. Through your belief in the goodness of every part, you have created a worldwide space for healing and hope. Thanks to you and the global IFS community's steadfast dedication, this model brings wholeness and peace to so many people. May God bless your compassionate hearts forever.

Dr. Steven Hayes, founder of *Acceptance and Commitment Therapy* (ACT). This pioneering work provides direction for this book and serves as a source of inspiration. Acceptance and Commitment Therapy has been a guiding beacon for my clients and me. It taught me that I experience peace in the acceptance, not the control, of thoughts and feelings. And where I practice acceptance, awareness, and engagement with my values, I can live a values-based life, even in the places that scare me. I thank you for this wonderful gift.

To **Dr. Stephen Porges** and the *Polyvagal* community: thank you so much for providing important scientific grounding. *Polyvagal Theory* has revolutionized our understanding of the nervous system's role in behavior and emotion. Through this incredible scientific work, I have a compassionate window through which to view the human condition: mine and others. I owe you my deepest gratitude.

To all of you who belong to the IFS and ACT global community, you give life and power to these transformative modalities, and I thank you from the bottom of my heart.

To the fellowship of *Adult Children of Alcoholics and Dysfunctional Families* (ACA), I offer my heartfelt thanks for providing the language, voice, and global network of healing. You point the way with integrity, generosity, and courage. It is a mighty spiritual fellowship that offers an opportunity for us all to reparent our inner children with authentic, spiritually gentle, leadership. Thank you for this incredible gift to humanity.

To the entire global healing community; past, present, and future: Thank you so much for walking this path and holding space so people have an opportunity to heal. I may not meet you in person, however, this road is shared and sacred. I know you by soul-recognition, and value your contributions immensely.

To Alice Rizzi, PsyD, Helen Dempsey-Henofer, LCSW, Josh Spell, MSW, LICSW, Michelle P. Maidenberg, Ph.D., MPH, LCSW-R, CGP, Loretta Crawford, RSW ECDCS CGP CCTP II, Carrie L. E. Wendt, Patricia L. Nunes, and Young Hee Chang, for your meticulous input and commitment to clarification of this book. I am deeply grateful for your encouragement, belief, and editorial contributions to this work. Together, you hold an energetic representation of **Edery House Press** - a planetary healing community that affirms compassion, evolution, and Self-empowered change. The book is our collective birthright, paying homage to the vibrant power within us.

And finally, for my beloved cousin, Leo Pollach, may your soul find eternal rest in God's loving embrace. You were an anchor in my life; your support provided a sanctuary, and your encouragement gave me direction. With you, I knew the meaning of a true family bond. Your sudden parting August 2024 has left an emptiness, a silence I now fill with cherished memories of our conversations, our shared laughter, and your unique wisdom. Thank you for being a fierce champion of my true self, a truth I will hold onto forever.

אני אוהבת אותך לעד - *I love you always, Leo.*

About The Author

Dr. Rivka Edery, Psy.D., LCSW, brings over fifteen years of expertise in trauma counseling to guide individuals toward healing and self-discovery. Through her innovative **The U Model™**, she empowers clients to transform past burdens into strengths by fostering internal self-leadership. **The U Model™** is a transformative approach that integrates Acceptance and Commitment Therapy (ACT) and Internal Family Systems Therapy (IFS).

The U Model™, transforms rigid inner parts by blending IFS's compassionate healing with ACT's action-oriented flexibility, guiding them from trauma-driven reactions to value-aligned adaptability. This integrated approach empowers individuals to harmonize their inner world and live with purpose.

As the author of *Trauma and Transformation: A 12-Step Guide* and founder of **Edery House Press**, Dr. Edery shares her groundbreaking approach with a global audience. Her creative, compassionate, evidence-based practice inspires clients to develop Self-leadership, the key to their healing.

Discover more at www.rivkaedery.com

MY REFLECTIONS

MY REFLECTIONS

MY REFLECTIONS

MY REFLECTIONS

Made in the USA
Monee, IL
12 October 2025

31054339R00060